COME OUT!

A Handbook for the Serious Deliverance Minister

By Jonas Clark

Unless otherwise noted, Scripture quotations are taken from the King James Version.

Come Out! A Handbook for the Serious Deliverance Minister
ISBN-10: 1-886885-10-9
ISBN-13: 978-1-886885-10-3

Published by Spirit of Life Publishing
27 West Hallandale Beach Blvd.
Hallandale, Florida
33009-5437, U.S.A.
(954) 456-4420

www.JonasClark.com

02 03 04 05 06 07 ¨ 07 06 05 04 03 02

ABOUT THE AUTHOR

Jonas Clark is a refreshing voice and a champion in the contemporary Church. Jonas served God for more than two decades as a pastor, teacher and evangelist before the Lord called him to his role as an apostle in the end time Church.

An evangelist at heart, Jonas travels around the world preaching the Gospel with a bold apostolic anointing. Fortitude and God's grace have taken his ministry into more than 25 countries, where he delivers a message of salvation, healing, deliverance and apostolic reformation. His passion is to win lost souls for Jesus Christ and equip every believer to take the Good News into the harvest fields to fulfill the Great Commission.

Jonas is the founder of The Global Cause Network, an international network of believers and Champion partners united to build a platform for the apostolic voice. He also heads Spirit of Life Ministries, a multi-cultural, non-denominational church in Hallandale Beach, Florida.

Jonas is the publisher of *The Voice* magazine, an online media platform that is Advancing Christian Life and Culture.

You can also watch him nationwide on the **Kingdom Living with Jonas Clark** television broadcast.

THIS BOOK IS DEDICATED TO:

All those who are not afraid to offer hope
to a desperate generation.

"For this purpose the Son of God was manifested, that he might destroy the works of the devil." (1 John 3:8 KJV)

CONTENTS

INTRODUCTION

As I have traveled throughout various countries of the world it is amazing to me just how often the ministry of deliverance is misunderstood. After a particular meeting some years ago, a devoted pastor asked me if I would pray for a young lady in his church who had been tormented for years by demons. He said that they had tried to cast the devils out of her for five years without success.

That night she walked away free from the powers of darkness.

This event showed me just how many good, well meaning and devoted saints there are who do not understand the power of the gospel of Jesus Christ to set the captives free.

In our modern society thousands are coming into our churches from the occult, witchcraft, spiritualism and the new age movement. They are going to need help from us that transcends any natural counseling abilities. This simply means that deliverance can no longer be ignored.

One of the main reasons that people do not "set the captives free" is a lack of knowledge of the scriptures and the authority given to them by Jesus in this area of ministry. It is my sincere desire to see people dramatically changed through the deliverance ministry. It is time for the church to exercise her authority against Satan who has been allowed to maintain his oppression without a challenge.

In this handbook we will learn...

- The scriptural foundation for deliverance
- How to continue the deliverance ministry of Jesus
- The different types of spirits mentioned in the Bible
- How to cast out devils
- Our authority as believers

- Six things evil spirits attach themselves to

- How to keep our deliverance.

From South Florida,

Your Partner,
Jonas Clark

Lesson 1

DOING THE WORKS OF JESUS

In this lesson we will discover our authority to do the works of Jesus.

One of the most fascinating aspects in the ministry of Jesus is deliverance. Nowhere in the Old Testament do you find such a demonstration of God's love for those whom Satan has bound. The word teaches us,

> "The reason the son of God appeared was to destroy the works of the devil" (1 John 3:8).

Before Jesus' public ministry to the nation of Israel, he was led by the Holy Spirit into the wilderness to be tempted and tried by Satan. In that desert place he prevailed and came out with power. His first stop was the church where he encountered a demon possessed man who spoke to him and said, *"Let us alone!"* Isn't it interesting that Jesus' first miracle *in the church* was deliverance? (Mark 1:21-27, Luke 4:31-36).

The advancement of the church of Jesus Christ cannot accomplish its mandate of world evangelism without challenging Satan's rule. When Jesus chose his apostles he saw in them revolutionaries that would impact their world with His great cause. When he called them he also gave them power to succeed.

> "And when he had called unto him his twelve disciples, he gave them power against unclean spirits, to cast them out, and to heal all manner of sickness and all manner of disease" (Matthew 10:1).

We too have been given power to succeed. One can never be effective in deliverance ministry until that person thoroughly understands their delegated authority as a believer. Authority is the power and right to give commands. Even if some do not believe that Jesus gave his disciples authority, the demons surely do. Jesus declared that we would do greater works than he.

> "Verily, verily, I say unto you, He that believeth on me, the *works* that I do shall he do also; and greater works than these shall he do; because I go unto my Father. (John 14:12, Italics added).

WHAT WERE THE WORKS OF JESUS?

Jesus' primary ministry as the only begotten Son of God was that of the Lamb of God that taketh away the sin of the world (John 1:29). There was and is only one Lamb of God who is Jesus our Messiah. He provided an atoning sacrifice for the sins of the world and offered himself as the *only* way of salvation and reconciliation to our Heavenly Father. Salvation is to all who would repent of their sins and believe that Jesus died and rose again.

In addition to these things that only Jesus could do, he demonstrated to us other aspects of ministry that we too, as believers, can do including...

- Teaching
- Preaching

- Healing
- Miracles
- Deliverance
- Intercession

These aspects of ministry belong to every child of God. They are the things that Jesus prophesied that we would do and even greater things (John 14:12).

AUTHORITY GIVEN TO EVERY BELIEVER

> "Behold, I give unto you power *(exousia)* to tread on serpents and scorpions, and over all the power *(dunamis)* of the enemy: and nothing shall by any means hurt you" (Luke 10:19, Italics added).

You can see in the above verse that the word power is actually two different Greek words. One word for power is *exousia,* meaning authority. The other word for power is *dunamis,* meaning mighty power. Unfortunately, the Bible translators did not help us understand this verse by translating both words as power. Jesus is literally saying in this verse,

> "Behold, I give unto you *authority* to tread on serpents and scorpions, and over all the power of the enemy: and nothing shall by any means hurt you."

So what is authority? Again, authority is the power or right to give a command! Serpents and scorpions are symbols of evil spirits of wickedness and demonic powers. Jesus identifies them as our enemy. So we learn that authority is...

- The power or right to command.
- The authorization to enforce obedience.
- The divine right to take action.
- The ability to make and execute final decisions.

The following are more scriptures that speak of authority given to every believer.

- **Authority To Teach All Nations**

> "And Jesus came and spake unto them, saying, All power is given unto me in heaven and in earth. Go ye therefore, and teach all nations, baptizing them in

the name of the Father, and of the Son, and of the Holy Ghost: Teaching them to observe all things whatsoever I have commanded you: and, lo, I am with you always, even unto the end of the world. Amen" (Matthew 28:18-20).

- **Authority To Heal The Sick**

"How God anointed Jesus of Nazareth with the Holy Ghost and with power: who went about doing good, and healing all that were oppressed of the devil; for God was with him" (Acts 10:38).

- **Authority Against Evil Spirits**

"And when he had called unto him his twelve disciples, he gave them power *(exousia)* against unclean spirits, to cast them out, and to heal all manner of sickness and all manner of disease." (Matthew 10:1)

- **Authority To Cast Out Devils**

"And as ye go, preach, saying, The kingdom of heaven is at hand. Heal the sick,

> cleanse the lepers, raise the dead, cast out devils: freely ye have received, freely give." (Matthew 10:7-8)

WHAT THE ANOINTING DOES

We must never lose sight of what the anointing actually does.

> "The Spirit of the Lord is upon me, because he hath anointed me to preach the gospel to the poor; he hath sent *(apostello)* me to heal the brokenhearted, to preach deliverance to the captives, and recovering of sight to the blind, to set at liberty them that are bruised, To preach the acceptable year of the Lord" (Luke 4:18-19).

The anointing has a definite purpose. Here are six major functions of the anointing...

1. Preach the gospel to the poor

2. Heal the brokenhearted

3. Deliverance to captives

4. Sight to the blind

5. Liberty to those who are bruised

6. God's favor and ministry of reconciliation

THE NAME OF JESUS BELONGS TO ALL BELIEVERS

Having the right to use the name of Jesus means that when you speak the word of God it is just as if Jesus himself were speaking. Wow!

So in the following scriptures we discover our rights as believers to command demon spirits to depart.

> "And these signs shall follow them that believe; In my name shall they cast out devils; they shall speak with new tongues" (Mark 16:17).

> "And this did she many days. But Paul, being grieved, turned and said to the spirit, I command thee in the name of Jesus Christ to come out of her. And he came out the same hour" (Acts 16:18).

DELIVERANCE IS BY THE SPIRIT OF GOD

Deliverance ministry is the operation of the Holy Spirit working together with a believer to set another free from demonic assignments. Apart from the operations of the loving grace of the Spirit of God, deliverance cannot be accomplished. From the following scriptures we learn of Jesus' heart to set the captives free.

- **By the Spirit of God**

> "But if I cast out devils by the Spirit of God, then the kingdom of God is come unto you" (Matthew 12:28).

> "But if I with the finger of God cast out devils, no doubt the kingdom of God is come upon you" (Luke 11:20).

- **By the Word of God**

> "When the even was come, they brought unto him many that were possessed with devils: and he cast out the spirits with

> *his* word, and healed all that were sick" (Matthew 8:16).

> "And they were astonished at his doctrine: for his word was with power *(exousia)*" (Luke 4:32).

COMMANDING AUTHORITY

I was working on the streets one day with an evangelistic team in one of the neighborhoods. There I met a young boy of about nine years old. He had been very unruly and tried to disrupt our efforts. Just after I arrived he came up to me sucking on a piece of candy and kicked at me. I raised my sunglasses, looked him directly in the eyes and prayed softly in tongues. Out of his mouth came these words, "leave *us* alone." Of course my response was, "Never!" He laughed and ran away. Jesus never taught his apostles to leave devils alone. In the following scriptures we see them speaking to him. Notice the plural use of the word us.

> "And there was in their synagogue a man with an unclean spirit; and he cried out, Saying, *Let us alone*; what have we to do with thee, thou Jesus of Nazareth? art thou come to destroy us? I know thee who thou art,

> the Holy One of God. And Jesus rebuked him, saying, Hold thy peace, and come out of him" (Mark 1:23-25 Italics added).

> "And they were astonished at his doctrine: for his word was with power. And in the synagogue there was a man, which had a spirit of an unclean devil, and cried out with a loud voice, Saying, *Let us alone*; what have we to do with thee, thou Jesus of Nazareth? art thou come to destroy us? I know thee who thou art; the Holy One of God. And Jesus rebuked him, saying, Hold thy peace, and come out of him. And when the devil had thrown him in the midst, he came out of him, and hurt him not" (Luke 4:32-35 Italics added).

The use of the word "us" teaches believers that there was more than one demon present. In the next lesson we will learn of at least twenty-seven demonic spirits that are mentioned in the word of God.

Lesson 2

SPIRITS MENTIONED IN THE BIBLE

In this lesson we will study some different spirits mentioned in the Bible.

As we pray deliverance for people we will often encounter various spirits. Many of these spirits are identifiable in the scriptures. The Bible speaks of at least twenty-seven. Let's take a look.

1. WICKED SPIRITS

The term spiritual wickedness in high places are those wicked spirits set on evil purposes, maliciousness, naughtiness and are just plain trouble makers.

> "For we wrestle not against flesh and blood, but against principalities, against powers, against the rulers of the darkness of this world, against spiritual wickedness in high places." (Ephesians 6:12)

2. SPIRIT OF JEZEBEL

The Bible speaks of a woman known as Jezebel, who attacked and killed the prophets of God, in the Old Testament (1 Kings 18:4). Then we see Jezebel's name mentioned again in the New Testament (Revelation 2:20). Obviously this cannot be the same woman that the Old Testament spoke of, but is rather the same spirit of Jezebel. We can conclude from this, that the spirit of Jezebel can live on, influence, and operate through others.

> "Notwithstanding I have a few things against thee, because thou sufferest that woman Jezebel, which calleth herself a prophetess, to teach and to seduce my servants to

> commit fornication, and to eat things sacrificed unto idols." (Revelation 2:20)

3. WOUNDED SPIRIT

This is one of the most common things needed in the body of Christ—deliverance from hurts and wounds. Apart from the anointing there is no freedom and little relief from inner hurts and wounds.

> "The spirit of a man will sustain his infirmity; but a wounded spirit who can bear?" (Proverbs 18:14)

This type of wound is an injury that is deep inside. It can often be caused by rejection, abuse or some other painful event. It can also be the result of a generational curse on the family.

4. SPIRIT OF OPPRESSION

The word speaks of a spirit that oppresses. When one feels oppressed things weigh heavy on their mind, they feel trampled down, distressed, over powered, subdued, troubled on every side, crushed and pressed down.

> "How God anointed Jesus of Nazareth with the Holy Ghost and with power: who went about doing good, and healing all that were *oppressed* of the devil; for God was with him." (Acts 10:38 Italics added)

5. SPIRIT OF BONDAGE

The Greek word for bondage is *doulein* which can be likened to the English word for a slave. A slave is one who is subject to the will of another. Many have been enslaved by a spirit of bondage.

> "For ye have not received the *spirit of bondage* again to fear; but ye have received the Spirit of adoption, whereby we cry, Abba, Father" (Romans 8:15 Italics added).

6. SORROWFUL SPIRIT

This is an almost uncontrollable sorrow. I saw this spirit in operation when a young four year old child drowned and the mother blamed herself.

> "And she was in bitterness of soul, and prayed unto the LORD, and wept sore." (1 Samuel 1:10)

7. SPIRIT OF FEAR

Fear is the weapon used to attack faith. The spirit of fear will paralyze you and cause you to make irrational decisions. I remember a precious lady who was delivered from a spirit of fear. She told me that she was always fearful of making decisions. She was also very uncomfortable stating her views when they were different than others. Today she is free!

> "For God hath not given us the *spirit of fear,* but of power, and of love, and of a sound mind" (2 Timothy 1:7 Italics added).

8. SPIRIT OF INSANITY

> "And when he went forth to land, there met him out of the city a certain man, which had devils long time, and ware no clothes, neither abode in any house, but in the tombs" (Luke 8:27).

9. SPIRIT OF DESPAIR

The word heaviness is from the Hebrew word *keheh* meaning dark, dim, depressed, weak, faint—despair. One in despair feels that there is no hope.

> "To appoint unto them that mourn in Zion, to give unto them beauty for ashes, the oil of joy for mourning, the garment of praise for the *spirit of heaviness;* that they might be called trees of righteousness, the planting of the LORD, that he might be glorified" (Isaiah 61:3 Italics added).

10. SPIRIT OF INJURY

Have you ever met someone that was prone to injury and accidents?

> "And oftentimes it hath cast him into the fire, and into the waters, to destroy him: but if thou canst do anything, have compassion on us, and help us. (Mark 9:22).

11. SPIRIT OF INFIRMITY

An infirmity is a weakness, disease or sickness. This spirit is commonly associated with causing sickness and even a strange fatigue. An infirmity can be a sickness (Luke 5:15), a disease (Luke 8:2), a crippling spirit or a physical malfunction (Luke 13:11).

> "And, behold, there was a woman which had a *spirit of infirmity* eighteen years, and

> was bowed together, and could in no wise lift up her-self" (Luke 13:11 Italics added).

> "When the even was come, they brought unto him many that were possessed with devils: and he cast out the spirits with his word, and healed all that were sick: That it might be fulfilled which was spoken by Esaias the prophet, saying, Himself took our infirmities, and bare our sicknesses" (Matthew 8:16-17).

12. SPIRIT OF SLUMBER

This spirit is fast at work blinding those who reject the truth of God.

> "For the LORD hath poured out upon you the spirit of deep sleep, and hath closed your eyes: the prophets and your rulers, the seers hath he covered" (Isaiah 29:10).

> "According as it is written, God hath given them the *spirit of slumber,* eyes that they should not see, and ears that they should not hear; unto this day" (Romans 11:8 Italics added).

13. SPIRIT OF JEALOUSY

To be jealous means to be resentfully envious of another. It causes one to be very suspicious of another's activities. King Saul was very jealous of David.

> "And Saul eyed (to look with an evil intent) David from that day and forward" (1 Samuel 18:9).

> "And the *spirit of jealousy* come upon him, and he be jealous of his wife, and she be defiled: or if the spirit of jealousy come upon him, and he be jealous of his wife, and she be not defiled" (Numbers 5:14 Italics added).

14. A PERVERSE SPIRIT

This is a spirit that perverts, confuses, twist, warps and distorts things. When this spirit operates, it causes one to walk in error. If you don't believe right then you can't think right. If you don't think right then you will continually make wrong decisions.

> "The LORD hath mingled a *perverse spirit* in the midst thereof: and they have caused

> Egypt to err in every work thereof, as a drunken man staggereth in his vomit" (Isaiah 19:14 Italics added).

Notice the fruit of a perverse spirit is error. This word err is the Hebrew word *taah* meaning to wander about physically and mentally, to go astray and to stagger.

15. SPIRIT OF DIVINATION

This is a very common spirit that loves to hang out in spirit-filled churches. Our generation must understand its operations and be careful to judge all prophetic operations.

> "And it came to pass, as we went to prayer, a certain damsel possessed with a *spirit of divination* met us, which brought her masters much gain by soothsaying" (Acts 16:16 Italics added).

16. A FAMILIAR SPIRIT

This spirit is one that is familiar with the details of a family. This spirit tries to deceive family members after the death of a love one with identical voices and personal details of a persons life. Speaking to the dead is strictly forbidden by God (Deuteronomy 18:10).

> "Then said Saul unto his servants, Seek me a woman that hath a *familiar spirit,* that I may go to her, and inquire of her. And his servants said to him, Behold, there is a woman that hath a familiar spirit at Endor. And Saul disguised himself, and put on other raiment, and he went, and two men with him, and they came to the woman by night: and he said, I pray thee, divine unto me by the familiar spirit, and bring me him up, whom I shall name unto thee." (1 Samuel 28:7-8 Italics added)
>
> (See also Deuteronomy 18:11, 2 Kings 23:24, Isaiah 8:9)

17. SPIRIT OF WHOREDOMS

The spirit of whoredoms can be seen in adultery, fornication, prostitution and idolatry. Homosexuality is also the working of this spirit. You can see this spirit operating as people are drawn into all sorts of sexual sins, flirting, inappropriate worldly dress, sexual sensuality and body movements.

> "...for the *spirit of whoredoms* hath caused them to err, and they have gone a whoring from under their God." (Hosea 4:12 Italics added)

18. A HAUGHTY SPIRIT

Pride is an excessive and unduly high opinion of oneself or ones accomplishments. To be haughty means to be lifted up.

> "Pride goeth before destruction, and an *haughty spirit* before a fall. {19} Better it is to be of an humble spirit with the lowly, than to divide the spoil with the proud" (Proverbs 16:18-19 Italics added).

19. LYING SPIRIT

This is probably the most common spirit found throughout the world and has caused countless troubles for people.

> "Now therefore, behold, the LORD hath put a *lying spirit* in the mouth of these thy prophets, and the LORD hath spoken evil against thee" (2 Chronicles 18:22 Italics added). (See also 1 Kings 22:21-23; 1 John 4:6)

20. ANTICHRIST SPIRIT

The word Christ means the anointed one. An antichrist spirit is just that—antichrist or anti-anointing. If he is antichrist and you are born again then he is anti-you. Scripture teaches us that there is an antichrist spirit fast at work in this world to buffet the Holy Spirit. It produces a disgust and contempt for the things of God.

> "And every spirit that confesseth not that Jesus Christ is come in the flesh is not of God: and this is that *spirit of antichrist,* whereof ye have heard that it should come; and even now already is it in the world" (1 John 4:3 Italics added).

> "Little children, it is the last time: and as ye have heard that antichrist shall come, even now are there many antichrists; whereby we know that it is the last time" (1 John 2:18).

21. UNCLEAN SPIRIT

I saw a news report of a woman who never took her garbage to the street. When they entered her home she had piles of rotting trash in every room stacked to the ceiling. This is the extreme of an unclean spirit.

The word unclean can also speak of one's thought life (Mark 5:8) that is continually tormented with perverse thinking. It can also speak of an unclean spirit in a territory (Zechariah 13:2).

> "For he said unto him, Come out of the man, thou *unclean* spirit" (Mark 5:8 Italics added).

22. DEAF & DUMB SPIRIT

The word speaks of a spirit that affects one's ability to hear and speak. This can also be seen in those who have speech impediments. In the following scripture Jesus speaks to this spirit.

> "Master, I have brought unto thee my son, which hath a dumb spirit; And wheresoever he taketh him, he teareth him: and he foameth, and gnasheth with his teeth, and pineth away: and I spake to thy disciples that they should cast him out; and they could not. He answereth him, and saith, O faithless generation, how long shall I be with you? how long shall I suffer you? bring him unto me. And they brought him unto him: and when he saw him, straightway the spirit tare him; and he

fell on the ground, and wallowed foaming. And he asked his father, How long is it ago since this came unto him? And he said, Of a child. And oftentimes it hath cast him into the fire, and into the waters, to destroy him: but if thou canst do anything, have compassion on us, and help us. Jesus said unto him, If thou canst believe, all things are possible to him that believeth. And straightway the father of the child cried out, and said with tears, Lord, I believe; help thou mine unbelief. When Jesus saw that the people came running together, he rebuked the foul spirit, saying unto him, Thou *dumb and deaf spirit,* I charge thee, come out of him, and enter no. more into him. And the spirit cried, and rent him sore, and came out of him: and he was as one dead; insomuch that many said, He is dead. But Jesus took him by the hand, and lifted him up; and he arose" (Mark 9:17-27 Italics added).

23. A MISLEADING SPIRIT

This scripture speaks of a spirit that misleads (*planos*) one into deception and corruption. It is very difficult for one to be deceived that has not been seduced. Notice e power of this spirit's ability to separate the righteous from a steadfast faith.

> "Now the Spirit speaketh expressly, that in the latter times some shall depart from the faith, giving heed to seducing *(planos)* spirits, and doctrines of devils" (1 Timothy 4:1).

24. SPIRIT OF ERROR

The spirit of error (Greek: *plane*) leads one astray from the right way by producing wrong thinking and actions. Error is the state of believing what is untrue, incorrect and wrong. It is a deviation from truth, accuracy, correctness or what's right.

> "We are of God: he that knoweth God heareth us; he that is not of God heareth not us. Hereby know we the spirit of truth, and the spirit of error *(plane)*" (1 John 4:6).

25. SPIRIT OF THE WORLD

The spirit of the world conforms people into a carnal, earthly minded state. They are drawn to worldly fashion, conversation, music, art and literature.

> "Now we have received, not the *spirit of the world,* but the spirit which is of God; that we might know the things that are freely given to us of God" (1 Corinthians 2:12 Italics added).

26. SPIRIT OF TREACHERY

Treachery is a betrayal of trust, faith or alliance. Those operating by this spirit are disloyal, give a false appearance of safety or reliability and will sell you out.

> "Then God sent an evil spirit between Abimelech and the men of Shechem; and the men of Shechem dealt treacherously with Abimelech" (Judges 9:23).

27. SPIRIT OF MURDER

> "And Saul cast the javelin; for he said, I will smite David even to the wall with it. And David avoided out of his presence twice" (1 Samuel 18:11)

> "And the evil spirit from the LORD was upon Saul, as he sat in his house with his javelin in his hand: and David played with his hand. And Saul sought to smite David

> even to the wall with the javelin; but he slipped away out of Saul's presence, and he smote the javelin into the wall: and David fled, and escaped that night. Saul also sent messengers unto David's house, to watch him, and to slay him in the morning: and Michal David's wife told him, saying, If thou save not thy life tonight, tomorrow thou shalt be slain" (1 Samuel 19:9-11).

In the next lesson we will learn of ten very important insights in deliverance ministry.

Lesson 3

TEN USEFUL INSIGHTS IN DELIVERANCE

In this lesson we will learn ten useful insights in deliverance.

It is vitally important for the deliverance minister not to look only to formulas, methodology or how-to's. The most important thing to understand as a deliverance minister is...

- One's authority as a believer.
- The scriptural foundations for deliverance.
- That guidance is provided by the Holy Spirit himself.

Deliverance is not a game or something to be played around with, but is a very serious matter that deals with the lives of precious people who need God's help.

Let's look at ten significant insights for the deliverance minister.

1. USE THE NAME OF JESUS

The name of Jesus is our most powerful weapon used for deliverance ministry. Jesus has given those who are born again divine right to use his name. As ambassadors of Christ (2 Corinthians 5:20) we have been duly authorized to use the name that all demons must obey.

An ambassador is the highest ranking diplomatic representative appointed by one country or government to represent another.

These two scriptures give us divine right to use the name of Jesus.

> "And these signs shall follow them that believe; In my name shall they cast out devils; they shall speak with new tongues." (Mark 16:17).

> "That at the name of Jesus every knee should bow, of things in heaven, and things in earth, and things under the earth" (Philippians 2:10).

2. DELIVERANCE IS BY THE SPIRIT OF GOD

> "But if I cast out devils by the Spirit of God, then the kingdom of God is come unto you." (Matthew 12:28)

Jesus told us that it was the Spirit of God who was involved in his deliverance ministry. Our relationship with the Holy Spirit working together with our faith in God is vitally important. Demons can never be talked out, negotiated out or manipulated out. You cannot make deals with demons. They have a ministry of destruction and must be cast out. The Greek word for cast out is *ekballo* meaning to...

- Violently drive out

- Expel by force.
- Command to depart.

3. THE GIFTS OF THE SPIRIT SHOULD ALWAYS BE OPERATIONAL DURING DELIVERANCE SESSIONS

The gifts of the Spirit are very important during deliverance sessions. Once we were praying for a woman who for years had been demonized. She had been abused as a child. Many others had prayed for her with some success but did not have a complete victory. They asked us to help her if we could. After spending quite some time with her in prayer and deliverance we came to an impasse. We had reached a dead end. Nothing was happening. It looked as if we had been defeated. We had done all that we knew to do. We desperately needed the precious gifts of the Holy Spirit if we were going to see victory. We diligently sought the Holy Spirit's guidance in prayer and he revealed to us by a word of knowledge and the discerning of spirits what to do next. Without his guidance this dear lady would have walked away with only minor relief. But the result was a complete deliverance for her.

The Lord has given to all believers various gifts of the Spirit that will come into operation during deliverance sessions. There are times when it will be an operation of a gift from the Holy Spirit that will reveal a specific key needed during a deliverance session.

> "For to one is given by the Spirit the word of wisdom; to another the word of knowledge by the same Spirit; To another faith by the same Spirit; to another the gifts of healing by the same Spirit; To another the working of miracles; to another prophecy; to another discerning of spirits; to another divers kinds of tongues; to another the interpretation of tongues" (1 Corinthians 12:8-10).

4. SPEAK THE WORD OFTEN DURING ELIVERANCE SESSIONS

> "When the even was come, they brought unto him many that were possessed with devils: and he cast out the spirits with *his* word, and healed all that were sick" (Matthew 8:16).

The word of God is not just one word. We should make every effort to know and peak the word of God during times of deliverance. It is the word of God that is a two-edged sword.

> "For the word of God is quick, and powerful, and sharper than any two-edged sword, piercing even to the dividing sunder of soul and spirit, and of the joints and marrow, and is a discerner of the thoughts and intents of the heart" (Hebrews 4:12).

5. USE YOUR COMMANDING AUTHORITY AS A BELIEVER

Jesus commanded spirits to leave and so can we. To command means to give an order that must be obeyed.

> "And they were all amazed, and spake among themselves, saying, What a word *is* this! for with authority and power he commandeth the unclean spirits, and they come out" (Luke 4:36).

6. THE ANOINTING REMOVES BURDENS AND DESTROYS THE YOKE OF BONDAGE

A burden is...

- a heavy weight load
- a care

....which someone is carrying around. It is heavy, cumbersome and a consuming weight. We can liken a yoke to a wooden bar fitted around the neck of two oxen and used to bind them together. Where one ox goes the other is forced to go too. Without the destruction of the yoke there is no separation from the bondage.

> "And it shall come to pass in that day, that his burden shall be taken away from off thy shoulder, and his yoke from off thy neck, and the yoke shall be destroyed because of the anointing" (Isaiah 10:27).

7. PLEAD THE BLOOD OF THE LAMB

The blood of Jesus is alive. When we plead the blood of Jesus during deliverance sessions demons tremble. They understand that the blood of Jesus speaks, redemption and deliverance for us, and eternal judgment for them.

> "And they overcame him by the blood of the Lamb, and by the word of their testimony; and they loved not their lives unto the death" (Revelation 12:11).

8. ANOINTED MUSIC

Music is one of the most powerful tools available to us as deliverance ministers. Often times I have seen people who were demonized walk out of services where anointed worship was present. I know the time is coming when mass deliverance will take place just through the worship of God alone. Let's look at some scriptural examples of music used in deliverance.

DAVID MINISTERS TO SAUL

When King Saul was being tormented by evil spirits David played music and Saul experienced some deliverance.

> "Let our lord now command thy servants, which are before thee, to seek out a man, who is a cunning player on an harp: and it shall come to pass, when the evil spirit from God is upon thee, that he shall play with his hand, and thou shalt be well" (1 Samuel 16:16).

> "And it came to pass, when the evil spirit from God was upon Saul, that David took an harp, and played with his hand: so Saul was refreshed, and was well,

> and the evil spirit departed from him" (1 Samuel 16:23).

This scripture teaches us three great the when we see what happened to the demonized King Saul as David played his harp.

1. Refreshing came.

2. Healing came.

3. Deliverance came.

When we worship God something powerful takes place! It...

- Exalts our Lord.

- Builds spiritual strength.

- Stills (ceases) the attacks of our enemies.

PRAISE STILLS THE AVENGER

The scripture teaches us that praise will cause the attacks of the enemy to cease. Praise is one of our greatest weapons of war.

> "Out of the mouth of babes and sucklings hast thou ordained strength [praise] because of thine enemies, that thou mightest still (cease) the enemy and the avenger" (Psalm 8:2, Matthew 21:16).

WEARING THE GARMENT OF PRAISE

Praising God releases us from the spirit of heaviness. A garment is clothing that we can by our own will put on or take off. Let us dress appropriately.

> "To appoint unto them that mourn in Zion, to give unto them beauty for ashes, the oil of joy for mourning, the garment of praise for the spirit of heaviness; that they might be called trees of righteousness, the planting of the LORD, that he might be glorified" (Isaiah 61:3).

9. ANOINTED CLOTHS

This seems to be one of the most unusual scriptures in the word of God dealing with deliverance. The anointing can be transferred into clothes and taken to the needy as the Apostle Paul demonstrated to the disciples in Ephesus.

> "...from his body were brought unto the sick handkerchiefs or aprons, and the diseases departed from them, and the evil spirits went out of them." (Acts 19:12)

10. PRAYER WITH GROANINGS

At times the deliverance minister self in a deep groaning type of prayer intercession. Spiritual groaning comes the very depths of one's spirit. To groan ring intercession is the Greek word *stenagmos* meaning a deep sigh. There are several scriptures that speak of groanings. Let's take a look at three of them.

INTERCESSION WITH GROANINGS

> "Likewise the Spirit also helpeth our infirmities: for we know not what we should pray for as we ought: but the Spirit itself maketh *intercession for us with groanings* which cannot be uttered." (Romans 8:26 Italics added)

The deliverance minister should always be open to the leading of the Holy Spirit to using different types of prayer, including groanings.

> "Praying always with all prayer and supplication in the Spirit, and watching thereunto with all perseverance and supplication for all saints" (Ephesians 6:18).

GROANINGS THAT RAISED THE DEAD

> "Jesus therefore again groaning in himself cometh to the grave. It was a cave, and a stone lay upon it" (John 11:38).

At Lazaras' grave we see Jesus groaning within himself. This word for groaning is from the Greek word *embrimaomai* meaning to sternly charge with an earnest command. I often wonder if Jesus had not been so specific when he called Lazarus by name to come forth out of that grave if everyone would not have been resurrected.

GROANINGS BRING DELIVERANCE

> "However, after a long time [nearly forty years] the king of Egypt died; and the Israelites were sighing and groaning because of the bondage. They kept crying, and their cry because of slavery ascended to God. And God heard their sighing and groaning and [earnestly) remembered His

> covenant with Abraham, with Isaac, and with Jacob." (Exodus 2:23-24 AMP)

In the next lesson we will explore deliverance events and the interesting association between healing and deliverance.

Lesson 4

HEALING AND DELIVERANCE

In this lesson we will review the scriptures that associate healing and deliverance.

Jesus tells the religious leaders about his deliverance and healing ministry..

> "The same day there came certain of the Pharisees, saying unto him, Get thee out, and depart hence: for Herod will kill thee. And he said unto them, Go ye, and tell

> that fox, Behold, *I cast out devils, and I do cures* today and tomorrow, and the third day I shall be perfected" (Luke 13:31-32 Italics added).

Scripture confirms that Jesus had a traveling deliverance ministry, and was anointed with the Holy Ghost and power healing all those who were oppressed by demons that came to him.

> "How God anointed Jesus of Nazareth with the Holy Ghost and with power: who went about doing good, and *healing all that were oppressed of the devil;* for God was with him" (Acts 10:38 Italics added).

It is very interesting to discover the close association between sickness and demon activity. The Apostle Paul had a deliverance ministry and even used handkerchiefs as tools for freedom.

> "So that from his body were brought unto the sick handkerchiefs or aprons, and the diseases departed from them, and the evil spirits went out of them" (Acts 19:12).

Jesus was well known to have a deliverance ministry. It seems everywhere he went the demonized and sick were brought to him and he set them free.

Let's read some scriptures that show us Jesus' deliverance ministry. Take note of the interesting association between healing and deliverance.

THOSE WITH DISEASES

> "Now when the sun was setting, all they that had any sick with divers diseases brought them unto him; and he laid his hands on every one of them, and healed them. And devils also came out of many, crying out, and saying, Thou art Christ the Son of God. And he rebuking them suffered them not to speak: for they knew that he was Christ" (Luke 4:40-41).

> "And at even, when the sun did set, they brought unto him all that were diseased, and them that were possessed with devils. And all the city was gathered together at the door. And he healed many that were sick of divers diseases, and cast out many devils; and suffered not the devils to speak, because they knew him" (Mark 1:32-34).

SPIRITS OF INFIRMITY

> "And, behold, there was a woman which had a spirit of infirmity eighteen years, and was bowed together, and could in no wise lift up herself. And when Jesus saw her, he called her to him, and said unto her, Woman, thou art loosed from thine infirmity. And he laid his hands on her: and immediately she was made straight, and glorified God" (Luke 13:11-13).

> "And ought not this woman, being a daughter of Abraham, whom Satan bath bound, lo, these eighteen years, be loosed from this bond on the sabbath day?" (Luke 13:16)

Even in the church Jesus cast out devils. A pattern we should still continue today.

> "And he preached in their synagogues throughout all Galilee, and cast out devils." (Mark 1:39)

DELIVERANCE IS THE CHILDREN'S BREAD

For years I have heard people misquote following scripture by saying that, "Healing was the children's bread." Actually the scripture teaches us that deliverance is the children's bread.

> "For a certain woman, whose young daughter had an unclean spirit, heard of him, and came and fell at his feet: The woman was a Greek, a Syrophenician by nation; and she besought him that he would cast forth the devil out of her daughter. But Jesus said unto her, Let the children first be filled: for it is not meet to take *the children's bread,* and to cast it unto the dogs. And she answered and said unto him, Yes, Lord: yet the dogs under the table eat of the children's crumbs. And he said unto her, For this saying go thy way; the devil is gone out of thy daughter. And when she was come to her house, she found the devil gone out, and her daughter laid upon the bed." (Mark 7:25-30 Italics added)

The Syrophenician woman's daughter had an unclean spirit. She came to Jesus out of desperation as any loving mother would. Jesus told her that deliverance belonged to the children of God first. This woman so impressed Jesus with her faith that he interceded for her daughter and the devil left her. Deliverance is the children's bread. It belongs to all who believe.

EXAMPLES OF DELIVERANCE

The story of Legion is one of the most encouraging testimonies of deliverance from demons in the Bible. Here we find a man so demonized that he was living among the tombs. But when the man saw Jesus he was able to run and worship the one who could set him free. Let's read the story.

LEGION

> "And when he was come out of the ship, immediately there met him out of the tombs a man with an unclean spirit, Who had his dwelling among the tombs; and no man could bind him, no, not with chains: Because that he had been often bound with fetters and chains, and the chains had been plucked asunder by him, and

the fetters broken in pieces: neither could any man tame him. And always, night and day, he was in the mountains, and in the tombs, crying, and cutting himself with stones. But when he saw Jesus afar off, he ran and worshipped him, And cried with a loud voice, and said, What have I to do with thee, Jesus, thou Son of the most high God? I adjure thee by God, that thou torment me not. For he said unto him, Come out of the man, thou unclean spirit. And he asked him, What is thy name? And he answered, saying, My name is Legion: for we are many. And he besought him much that he would not send them away out of the country. Now there was there nigh unto the mountains a great herd of swine feeding. And all the devils besought him, saying, Send us into the swine, that we may enter into them. And forthwith Jesus gave them leave. And the unclean spirits went out, and entered into the swine: and the herd ran violently down a steep place into the sea, (they were about two thousand;) and were choked in the sea." (Mark 5:2 13)

LESSONS FROM LEGION

1. He was territorial
2. He could not be tamed
3. He could not be restrained
4. He cried out (screamed) with a loud voice
5. He cut himself with stones
6. He was able to run to Jesus

Notice that devils do not want to be sent out of their territory. A legion *(legeon)* is a body of soldiers whose numbers vary. In the time of Augustus they consisted of 6826 men (6100 foot soldiers and 726 horsemen).

In this demonically dominated territory the people wanted Jesus to leave. Jesus said to the man, "Go home to your friends and tell them what the Lord has done" (Mark 5:19). Jesus gave him a testimony.

MARY MAGDALENE

Mary Magdalene is one of the most distinguished women in the New Testament. The first appearance of her is in the gospels in Luke 8:2 where she is found ministering to Jesus. Mary so loved the Lord that she was honored by the Lord to be the first witness of his resurrection. Mary had seven devils cast out of her.

> "Now when Jesus was risen early the first day of the week, he appeared first to Mary Magdalene, out of whom he had cast seven devils" (Mark 16:9).

DELIVERANCE IS A MIRACLE MINISTRY

> "And John answered him, saying, Master, we saw one casting out devils in thy name, and he followeth not us: and we forbade him, because he followeth not us. But Jesus said, Forbid him not: for there is no man which *shall do a miracle in my name,* that can lightly speak evil of me" (Mark 9:38-39 Italics added).

Jesus himself refers to deliverance ministry as being the working of a miracle *(semeion)* in his name. Philip also flowed in a miracle deliverance ministry.

> "And the people with one accord gave heed unto those things which Philip spake,

hearing and *seeing the miracles* which he did. For unclean spirits, crying with loud voice, came out of many that were possessed with them: and many taken with palsies, and that were lame, were healed." (Acts 8:6-7 Italics added)

Notice what the miracles were...

- Unclean spirits came out of many
- Those with palsies and those lame were healed.

The word miracle *(semeion)* means...

- A sign
- A mark
- A token
- An unusual occurrence
- something that transcends the common course of nature.

In the next lesson we will answer the question, "How do we know if someone needs deliverance?"

Lesson 5

WHO NEEDS DELIVERANCE?

In this lesson we will answer the question, "Who needs deliverance?"

We should begin this lesson with a note of caution. None of us know everything there to know about deliverance ministry, yet we have learned a few things from experience. We can learn from someone else's experience, but we should never use experience only as doctrine. Let's look now at two reasons to pray deliverance for someone. The first reason to pray deliverance for someone is because deliverance belongs to us and is provided in the atonement. The second is that deliverance will enable one have a closer walk with the Lord.

Over the years most of the people that I have met knew without any doubt that they needed deliverance. There always seemed be some reoccurring thing that kept causing them problems. Perhaps though some deliverance candidates are not really sure So let's consider the following items to discover if deliverance is needed.

SICKNESS

We have already looked at the close association between sickness and deliverance. (Acts 10:38; Luke 13:11; Matthew 8:16-17)

EMOTIONAL AND MENTAL PROBLEMS

Continual emotional ups and downs are sometimes indications of demonic activity. Fear, worry, undue concern, instability, mind traffic, depression, anger, rage, rejection, insecurity, confusion, loss of memory, torment, imaginations.

SEXUAL PROBLEMS

Lust, fornication, adultery, homosexuality, incest, masturbation, timidity, uncleanness.

ADDICTIONS

Prescription drugs, Illegal drugs, alcohol, nicotine, food.

OCCULT INVOLVEMENT

False religions, masons, yoga, mind sciences, Mormonism, séances, witchcraft, magic, Satanism, horoscopes, psychic readings.

GENERATIONAL CURSES

Obvious generational curses against one's life and family.

WHERE ARE DEMONS LOCATED?

Demons can reside in all three areas of a person.

- Spirit
- Soul

- Body

> "And the very God of peace sanctify you wholly; and I pray God your whole spirit and soul and body be preserved blameless unto the coming of our Lord Jesus Christ." (1 Thessalonians 5:23)

From this scripture we learn that mall was created by God a three part being.

1. The spirit of man is that part of marl which gets born again. He is the new creature. He is that part of man that contacts and fellowships with God.

> "Therefore if any man be in Christ, he is a *new creature*: old things are passed away; behold, all things are become new" (2 Corinthians 5:17 Italics added).

2. The soul of man is the mind, will, intellect, reasoning, imaginations and emotions. This is the part of man that continually needs to be renewed. This part of man is being sanctified daily.

> "And be not conformed to this world: but be ye transformed by the renewing of your mind, that ye may prove what is that good,

> and acceptable, and perfect, will of God" (Romans 12:2).

3. The body of man is that physical natural body that touches the physical world.

WE ARE NO LONGER UNDER SATAN'S AUTHORITY

It is extremely important to understand at the day we were born again is the day at we came out from under the authority darkness. The Bibles teaches that we have been translated.

> "Giving thanks unto the Father which hath made us meet to be partakers of the inheritance of the Saints in light: who hath delivered us from the power [authority] of darkness and hath *translated* us into the kingdom of his dear Son: In whom we have redemption [ransom, & full deliverance] through his blood even the forgiveness of sins." (Colossians 1:12-14 Italics added)

The definition of *translated* means to be moved from one place to another. So we learn to be translated means to be transferred...

- From darkness to light.
- From bondage to freedom.
- From demonic rulership to Holy Spirit liberty.

When one is born again he is translated from the realm of the *authority* of darkness into the loving kingdom of Jesus Christ the Son of God.

The next study will reveal some very important information on how demons attach themselves to people. Remember during deliverance sessions we must take the devil's rights away from him.

Lesson 6

SIX THINGS EVIL SPIRITS ATTACH THEMSELVES TO

In this lesson we will discover six things that evil spirits attach themselves to.

Evil spirits know their rights. When given the opportunity demons can gain legal entry into a person's life to bring torment. The first and most powerful license for demonic activity is sin.

1. SIN

"Giving thanks unto the Father, which hath made us meet to be partakers of the inheritance of the saints in light: Who hath delivered us from the power of darkness, and hath translated us into the kingdom of his dear Son: In whom we have redemption through his blood, even the forgiveness of sins" (Colossians 1:12-14).

Sin is separation from God. When one sins he...

- Gives the enemy a foot-hold
- Is in danger of giving demonic powers a right to attack
- Opens a door for demonic assignments.

2. BITTERNESS & UNFORGIVENESS

"And his lord was wroth, and delivered him to the tormentors, till he should pay all that was due unto him. So likewise shall my heavenly Father do also unto you, if ye from your hearts forgive not

> everyone his brother their trespasses" (Matthew 18:34-35).

This scripture is very clear that we must guard our own hearts from unforgiveness. When we choose not to forgive those who hurt us that unforgiveness opens the door for tormenting spirits.

3. HURTS & WOUNDS

> "The spirit of a man will sustain his infirmity; but a wounded spirit who can bear?" (Proverbs 18:14)

This is one of the most common deliverances seen when prayer is offered for an individual at the altar during services. Thousands of people are set free from hurts and wounds. Many have told me that they were instantly healed by the power of the Holy Spirit from years of hurts that seemed o be buried alive deep within them when I prayed for them. It is so wonderful to see people set free from years of hurt and pain.

4. CONTRACTS, AGREEMENTS

> "Thou shalt make no covenant with them, nor with their gods. They shall not dwell in thy land, lest they make thee sin against

> me: for if thou serve their gods, it will surely be a snare unto thee" (Exodus 23:32-33).

> "Take heed to thyself, lest thou make a covenant with the inhabitants of the land whither thou goest, lest it be for a snare in the midst of thee" (Exodus 34:12).

Demons are always looking for someone to make an agreement with them. Whether knowingly or unknowingly the devil will attempt to get you to enter into a contract with him.

> A contract is a binding agreement between two or more parties.

When I was in Africa I prayed one night for a demon possessed women who had the night before given her life to Jesus. This night was quite different indeed. We battled with a demon spirit that repeatedly told me that she belonged to him. I rebuked the evil spirit and asked the lady to renounce any contracts or agreements that she had made with this demon. She repented of her sin of making an agreement with him and God set her free. Later she told me that she had gone home after the previous nights service and was awakened in the night by a demon who was demanding his property. She told me that she was the property. I was bit perplexed. She continued to tell me the story. Apparently she was very poor and needed money to support her family. So she went down to the river and made a vow to some water god that if he would help then she would serve him. She then jumped into the river and it was then that evil spirit entered her. She told me that for years she regretted what she did and was tormented with grievous sores that would break out on her body. Oh how dangerous it is to make an agreement with demonic powers. Fortunately this woman was set free!

5. CURSES

The scriptures teach of generational ,es that attempt to follow down family trees.

> "Keeping mercy for thousands, forgiving iniquity and transgression and sin, and that will by no means clear the guilty; visiting the iniquity of the fathers upon the children, and upon the children's children, unto the third and to the fourth generation." (Exodus 34:7)

> "Thou shalt not bow down thyself unto them, nor serve them: for I the LORD thy

God am a jealous God, visiting the iniquity of the fathers upon the children unto the third and fourth generation of them that hate me" (Deuteronomy 5:9).

6. IDOLS

"Thou shalt have no other gods before me." (Exodus 20:3)

Idolatry is anything that you put before God. It is the worship of something other than our Creator himself. Idolatry may not include the bowing down to a statue but the replacement of God with something else in the heart and mind of the believer. Idolatry appears to be among the greatest temptations our spiritual forefathers faced. Moreover idolatry is so strictly forbidden that even their images (photographs) were forbidden (Exodus 20:4-6).

Our God is a jealous God and will not tolerate idolatry in his midst. Examples of idols mentioned in the word of God include the following.

- Abraham's father served idols (Joshua 24:2)
- Household idols (Genesis 31:34)
- Golden calf at Sinai (Exodus 32:14)

- Moab idols at Baal of Peor (Numbers 25:1-3)
- A city given to idolatry (Acts 17:16)
- Covetousness (greedy desires) (Colossians 3:5)

Many of God's prophets spoke out boldly against idolatry. (Isaiah 2:8; Jeremiah 50:2; Ezekiel 6:4-6; Micah 1:7; Habakkuk 2:18; and Zechariah 13:2). The question still prevails today, "Whom will you serve?" (Joshua 24:15-16). We must be careful not to give the devil anything to attach himself to.

In the next lesson we will discover five very important keys to deliverance.

Lesson 7

FIVE KEYS IMPORTANT TO DELIVERANCE

In this lesson we will look at five major keys to deliverance.

Since evil spirits enter a person's life legally, *ie.* with one's permission, either knowingly or unknowingly through deception or ignorance. They will battle to keep their rightful place in an individual's life, therefore every deliverance minister must be astute in the following vital steps to minster deliverance.

1. DEEP REPENTANCE

The deliverance minister must remember that there is no foundation for deliverance without repentance.

Deep repentance is the first key for successful deliverance sessions.

> "Yet I am glad now, not because you were pained, but because you were *pained into repentance* [that turned you to God]; for you felt a grief such as God meant you to feel, so that in nothing you might suffer loss through us or harm for what we did. For godly grief and the pain God is permitted to direct, produce a repentance that leads and contributes to salvation and deliverance from evil, and it never brings regret; but worldly grief (the hopeless sorrow that is characteristic of the pagan world) is deadly [breeding and ending in death]" (2 Corinthians 7:9-10 AMP, Italics added).

We have found that most deliverance candidates' understanding of repentance is superficial at best. Repentance is more than just saying that you are sorry.

The deliverance candidate must be brought to see the utter sinfulness of their particular sin. To repent means to turn from your wicked ways.

> Prolonged deliverance sessions often point to a shallow repentance on the part of the deliverance candidate.

All deliverance candidates need to be led into "deep repentance." This may take some teaching on what repentance really is along with an hour of prayer just repenting of sin.

They need to become aware of how utterly sinful their sin is and how they grieve the heart of God. It is godly sorrow that produces repentance.

> "For godly sorrow worketh repentance to salvation not to be repented of: but the sorrow of the world worketh death" (2 Corinthians 7:10).

2. FORGIVENESS

> "And his Lord was wroth, and delivered him to the tormentors, till he should pay all that was due unto him. So likewise

> shall my heavenly Father do also unto you, if ye from your hearts forgive not everyone his brother their trespasses" (Matthew 18:34-35).

The tormentors are those who...

- Torture.
- Bring pain.
- Anguish.
- Agony.
- Harassment.

Forgiveness is the second major key to casting out demonic powers. We must get rid of a demon's right to be present.

> "And when ye stand praying, forgive, if ye have ought against any: that your Father also which is in heaven may forgive you your trespasses. But if ye do not forgive, neither will your Father which is in heaven forgive your trespasses" (Mark 11:25-26).

3. RENOUNCING

To renounce means to give up, cast off, disown, or to refuse further association with. Because Satan knows his rights he will accuse you before God of having a binding contract or agreement with him. We must be sure to verbally renounce any of these legal associations we made with the devil either knowingly and unknowingly:

- Covenants.
- Contracts.
- Agreements.

4. REMOVING

We also must remove Satan's property from our possession such as...

- Demonic jewelry.
- Art work.
- Books.
- Films/videos.

- Computer files.

You cannot cast out demons if they have a right to be present. Having possession of their property gives them the right to be present. We must remove their rights. Don't hold on to anything. Everything must go!

Once I prayed for a precious young lady who was being tormented by demon spirits at night. I told her that I would pray with her every day until she was totally free. Praying for her was very difficult. Daily the battles seemed to rage with every kind of manifestation one could imagine. After the third day in my private time of prayer I was asking the Holy Spirit why we were not having the full success that we should be seeing. The Holy Spirit showed me that even after I had told her to get rid of any demonic objects that she had in her possession that there was still one remaining. The next day I met with the young lady and told her what the Holy Spirit had said to me. She began to cry and through tears told me that she was not willing to give up the demonic object. I pleaded with her to no avail. The deliverance session was over.

The last time I saw her she was somewhat psychotic, came into the church with bongos strapped to her waste and told one of our ushers that God had called her to lead the praise and worship that service. She had sunk even deeper into demonic possession. My heart still goes out to her and particularly her precious mother and very young daughter.

5. CRYING OUT TO GOD

Crying out to God for help is one of the most powerful dynamics in deliverance. Many times during deliverance we have people cry out to Jesus to help them.

> "However, after a long time [nearly forty years] the king of Egypt died; and the Israelites were sighing and groaning because of the bondage. They kept crying, and their cry because of slavery [bondage] ascended to God. And God heard their sighing and groaning and [earnestly] remembered His covenant with Abraham, with Isaac, and with Jacob." (Exodus 2:23-24 AMP)

In the next lesson we will study some misconceptions about deliverance including the often misunderstood word 'possession.'

Lesson 8

POSSESSED OR DEMONIZED?

In this lesson we will study the meaning of the term possession.

There are some misconceptions in deliverance ministry regarding the difference between possession and being demonized. Can a demon take complete control of a person? Let's take a look.

> "When the even was come, they brought unto him many that were possessed with devils: and he cast out the spirits with

his word, and healed all that were sick."
(Matthew 8:16)

DEMONIZED

In the above scripture they brought to Jesus those who were possessed with devils. The Greek word for possess is *daimonizomai* meaning to be...

- Vexed.
- Troubled.
- Distressed.
- Afflicted.
- Plagued.
- Agitated.

The word possessed is one of the most misunderstood words in regards to deliverance ministry. It is essential that we understand that the word possessed in the above text means literally...

- To be demonized.

The English understanding of the word possessed means to be totally under the control of demon powers, but in scripture the word possessed is properly understood to be...

- Demonized vexed.
- Tormented oppressed troubled.

So we learn by this that a person can be demonized and not be out of control.

MAN'S FREE WILL

God has given all of us a free will that the devil can never take away from us. If we were totally possessed and under the supreme control of demon powers, then God could not judge us for our sin and remain a just judge.

The scripture says that evening had come and they brought those who were demonized *(daimonizomai)* to Jesus (Matthew 8:16). The question arises, "Where were these people in the day time?" I submit to the reader that most were at work or about their normal daily activities. Therefore even though they were possessed *(daimonizomai)* they still had the ability to function (to varying degrees) on a daily basis. I have seen countless numbers of demonized people come to the altar for deliverance. They still were able to fully exercise their will to come to Jesus for help.

ONE WORD?

Once I cast a demon out of a lady at the altar during one of the services. That demon was really stubborn and struggled to stay. I repeatedly commanded it to come out which it finally did. After the service I was challenged by a young man with a religious spirit who said that Jesus cast out demons by using one word. The suggestion was that I was out of order by repeatedly commanding that thing to come out. I asked him how many demons he had cast out. He turned red and left the building.

Surely you too have heard someone say the same thing, "Jesus cast out demons with just one word." However scripture does not support that statement. Let's take a look at the scripture they are referring to.

> "... and he cast out the spirits with *his* word, and healed all that were sick" (Matthew 8:16).

Notice that Jesus cast out these spirits with his word. First of all the scripture does not say one word but rather his word. The his being italicized means that the word his was added by the Bible translators and is not in the original Greek. Therefore this does not mean that Jesus cast out spirits with one single word. I speak the word each week during our church services at Spirit of Life Ministries in Hallandale Florida, but I speak more than one word when I do speak.

INSTANTLY OUT?

It is also stated many times that demons should come out with just one single command of, "Come out!" Anyone who has spent anytime in deliverance ministry knows this to be entirely untrue. I have seen demons come out with just one command, however it is not the norm. One word or one hundred words, let's help people get free. Amen? If one, "Come out!" doesn't work, don't stop, keep going.

Yes, I believe that the day is coming when the anointing will be so strong that one, "Come out" will be sufficient. But until that day comes don't stop commanding until that demon gives up the battle and leaves.

THE SAME HOUR

> "And this did she many days. But Paul, being grieved, turned and said to the spirit, I command thee in the name of Jesus Christ

> to come out of her. And he came out the *same hour.*" (Acts 16:18 Italics added)

We can learn from this scripture reference to "the same hour." It does not mean deliverance was seen at the very instant that the command to leave was given. We learn that this spirit came out that same hour or *within* an hour. The important lesson to learn is that the evil spirit in fact came out.

Paul also tells us of wrestling with demonic powers (Ephesians 6:12). A wrestling match is...

> Combat between two opposing forces.

I submit that one should wrestle until the demonic forces give up and leave. Even if it requires more than one command of, "Come out!" In the next lesson we will study the ways to keep one's deliverance.

Lesson 9

HOW TO KEEP YOUR DELIVERANCE

In this lesson we will study twelve truths that will help one keep their deliverance.

Demons desire a human habitation. They find no rest in a disembodied state and wonder about seeking a person they can inhabit. Demons that have been cast out will keep a watchful eye for an opportunity to return to those from whom they have been evicted. Unless we do something to keep the demon out he will try to come back to his former residence. But when he returns he will be accompanied by seven spirits more wicked than himself. Don't let this frighten you because Jesus has made provision to handle this. After a person gets deliverance it is vitally important for that person to be filled with the Holy Spirit.

1. BE FILLED WITH THE HOLY SPIRIT

> "Then he saith, I will return into my house from whence I came out; and when he is come, he findeth it empty, swept, and garnished. Then goeth he, and taketh with him-self seven other spirits more wicked than himself, and they enter in and dwell there: and the last state of that man is worse than the first. Even so shall it be also unto this wicked generation." (Matthew 12:44-45)

After Jesus' resurrection, he commanded his disciples not to depart from Jerusalem, but to wait for the promise of the Father. Jesus had spoken of this same promise when he said, "If you love me, keep my commandments. And I will pray the Father, and he shall give you another Comforter, that he may abide with you forever, even the Spirit of truth; whom the world cannot receive, because it seeth him not, neither knoweth him: but you know him; for he dwelleth with you, and shall be in you" (John 14:15-17).

Jesus declared, "For John truly baptized with water; but you shall be baptized with the Holy Ghost not many days hence." Jesus also told them that they would "receive power after that the Holy Ghost was come upon them and at they would be witnesses unto him" (Acts 1:4-8).

> "And when the day of Pentecost was fully come, they were all with one accord in one place, and suddenly there came a sound from heaven as of a rushing mighty wind, and it filled all the house where they were sitting. And there appeared unto them cloven tongues like as of fire, and it sat upon each of them. And they were all filled with the Holy Ghost, and began to speak with other tongues, as the Spirit gave them utterance" (Acts 2:1-4).

PRAYER FOR BAPTISM

Let's pray together. Jesus, thank you that you are my Lord and my Savior. Lord I want everything that you have to give me. I desire deep within me the precious gift of the Holy Spirit that you poured out on your servants in the upper room. By faith and according to your word, baptize me and fill me right now with this same power from on high. Thank you, Lord!

2. GET WATER BAPTISM

If you have never been water baptized you should do so. Water baptism is a public profession of faith. It is your testimony that you have repented of your sins and have surrendered your life to Jesus.

> "He that believeth and is baptized shall be saved; but he that believeth not shall be damned." (Mark 16:16)

> (See also Matthew 3:6, 13-16, Acts 2:38-41, 8:12, 36-38, 9:18, 10:47-48, 16:15,33, 18:8, 22:16)

3. PUT ON THE ARMOR OF GOD

Putting on the full armor of God is very important to every believer. The word teaches us that God allows us to wear his armor that we might be able to withstand, resist and oppose any demonic force arrayed against us. His armor is made up of seven pieces. Let's take a look.

1. Stand with the belt of truth about our loins. (Ephesians 5:9; Jeremiah 1:17; Luke 12:35; 1 Peter 1:13)

2. The breastplate of righteousness. (Jeremiah 23:6; Acts 24:16; 1 Thessalonians 5:8)

3. Feet shod with the preparation (readiness) of the gospel of peace. (Deuteronomy 33:25; Isaiah 52:7; Romans 10:15; 2 Corinthians 5:18-21)

4. The shield of faith that extinguishes the attacks of demon spirits. (Genesis 15:1; Psalm 56:3-11; Proverbs 18:10; 1 Peter 6:1-9; 1 John 5:45)

5. Helmet of salvation that protects our mind from every vain imagination and reassures us that we belong to Jesus. (Isaiah 59:17; Psalm 27:1; Hebrews 6:17-19)

6. Tightly griping the sword of the Spirit which is speaking the word of God. It is our only offensive weapon.
(Matthew 4:4; Hebrews 4:12; 2 Corinthians 10:4; Revelations 12:11)

7. Praying in the Spirit (unknown tongues). This is not our only way of praying. But praying in the spirit is directly associated with God's battle clothes.
(John 4:24; 1 Corinthians 14:2, 14; Acts 1:8, 2:4, 19:6)

Not only should we study about the various pieces of the armor of God but we need to apply that armor through prayer. Here is a prayer to apply the armor.

PRAYING ON THE ARMOR OF GOD

Thank you Jesus that you are allowing me to wear your armor. With this prayer of faith I am putting on the armor that you have given me the right to wear. Right now I gird my loins with gospel truth. For your word lights my life and my path. By your word of truth I know that I am walking in the right direction. I put on the

> breastplate of righteousness recognizing that I have been accepted by you. I step into my gospel shoes because I am ready to share the good news that Jesus died on the cross for my sins. I have repented of all sins and asked Jesus into my life forever. Jesus is Lord and captain of my life. I am a child of God, prepared and ready to spread the good news of the gospel of peace to others. I grab hold of the shield of faith because I know that by faith it will put out, extinguish all demonic attacks against me. I walk by faith and not by sight. Thank you Jesus for the helmet of salvation. By faith I put it on my head to guard my mind from vain imaginations that the enemy would try to inflict upon me. I lay hold and grip tightly the sword of the Spirit and stand ready to speak your word with boldness. And finally God I thank you for who you are, my strong tower and my mighty warrior. Amen.

After you have said this prayer then praise God for who he is and then pray in tongues. Remember that when you pray in tongues that is your spirit is praying to God. That is your heavenly prayer language.

4. MAINTAIN FAITH IN GOD

> "For whatsoever is born of God overcometh the world: and this is the victory that overcometh the world, even our faith." (1 John 5:4)

Every believer must develop a strong trust in the Lord. Faith is simply believing and trusting in God and demonstrating that trust with faithful actions. Trust is a confidence in the integrity and reliability of God. Trust holds fast to a confident expectation and anticipation of hope. "Now faith is the Substance of things hoped for, the evidence things not seen" (Hebrews 11:1). All believers must resist doubt and unbelief at all cost. Unbelief is the thief that attacks every believer.

5. RESIST THROUGH SUBMISSION

The word teaches us to submit to God (first), resist the devil and he will flee.

> "Submit yourselves therefore to God. Resist the devil, and he will flee from you." (James 4:7)

One way to resist the devil is through submission. The opposite of submission is rebellion. Rebellion opens the door for demon powers to gain entrance. Rebellion against God's word or those who have positions of spiritual authority over you can open the door for demonic activity. For example teenage children need to understand the importance of the spiritual covering of protection that is provided by submitting to loving and godly parents.

Oftentimes I see people who come into a demonic warfare or some great personal trial run from their pastors whom God has spiritually equipped to help protect them. A shepherd carries a rod and a staff. The rod is used to attack any predators that may try and harm the sheep and the staff is used to lead the sheep into green pastures.

At other times people will skirt the real issues, tell half truths and mislead their leaders. I have had others who told me that I was their pastor but yet refused to seek my counsel and years of experience through walking with God because they knew that I would not agree with their actions (rebellion).

Godly leaders are God's gift to the body of Christ (Ephesians 4:11). Don't run from God's word, God's leaders or God's church. To submit means to yield your will to another. Here are six important submission scriptures.

1. to God (James 4:7)
2. to each other (Ephesians 5:21)
3. to own husbands (Ephesians 5:22)
4. to rulers (1 Peter 2:13-14)
5. to elders (Greek: *presbuteros*) (1 Peter 5:5)
6. to godly Christian leaders (Hebrews 13:17)

Stay away from dead, dumb churches. Plug into a strong local church that understands deliverance. Don't go to a dead, formal and carnal church that has no spiritual understanding of demonic activity. (See also Matthew 26:39, 42; Mark 14:36; Hebrews 5:8; 10:5)

6. STAY AWAY FROM THE OLD PLACES

It is vital to stay away from those places where you are enticed to sin. Don't go back on the devil's territory. I remember when I was baptized with the Holy Spirit. I was so excited about what the Lord had done for me that I got in my car and was driving to Miami to see my unsaved friends. I was ready to share my testimony with them and help them "see the light." While I was driving I heard the Holy Spirit speak to me and ask,

> "Will you go back down to Egypt without consulting me?"

Needless to say, I turned the car around and headed back home. I had been acting out of a zeal for God without direction from the Holy Spirit. I learned a powerful lesson that day. Not every good action is a right action.

7. WATCH YOUR ASSOCIATIONS

Wrong associations are very dangerous and can do more damage than Satan himself.

> "For if after they have escaped the pollutions of the world through the knowledge of the Lord and Saviour Jesus Christ, they are again entangled therein, and overcome, the latter end is worse with them than the beginning. For it had been better for them not to have known the way of righteousness, than, after they have known it, to turn from the holy commandment delivered unto them. But it is happened unto them according to the true proverb, The dog is turned to his own vomit again; and the sow that was washed to her wallowing in the mire." (2 Peter 2:20-22)

8. BUILD YOURSELF UP IN WORD AND SPIRIT

Praying in tongues is the scriptural way to build and strengthen your spirit man (Jude 1:20). Not only should we be praying in tongues but we should also develop a discipline by spending time daily in prayer and the study of the word of God. Prayer and time in the word are equally important.

> "And be not conformed to this world: but be ye transformed by the renewing of your mind, that ye may prove what is that good, and acceptable, and perfect, will of God" (Romans 12:2).

9. BE AN OVERCOMER

> "And they overcame him by the blood of the Lamb, and by the word of their testimony; and they loved not their lives unto the death" (Revelation 12:11).

Every believer can be an overcomer. The Greek word for overcomer is nikao meaning to carry off the victory. This powerful scripture demonstrates four principles needed to keep one's deliverance.

1. "they overcame him by the blood of the Lamb."

The *him* represents Satan and all demonic forces. Because of Jesus' blood we can overcome meaning to carry off the victory. Believers have redemption through the blood of Jesus and the forgiveness of sins (Ephesians 1:7). Not only does the blood of Jesus redeem us from our sins but it seals the fate of demon powers and also signifies their coming judgment. Pleading the blood of Jesus over our life and against demon powers reminds them of a pending judgment in a lake of eternal fire for...

The beast and false prophet (Revelation 19:20).

The devil (Revelation 20:10).

Death and hell (Revelation 20:14).

Those whose names are not in the book of life (Revelation 20:15).

2. "by the word of their testimony."

I can't stress enough the importance of being able to share your personal testimony. Every new born believer or person who has received deliverance should be able to articulate their personal testimony. Jesus said,

> "Go home to your friends, and tell them about the great things the Lord has done for you, and has had compassion on you" (Mark 5:19).

3. "loved not their lives."

Jesus said, "If any man will come after me, let him deny himself, and take up his cross, and follow me" (Matthew 16:24). To deny ourselves literally means to lose sight our own selfish interest. Jesus must be Lord of our lives.

4. "unto death."

Believers should have such a love for God that they are willing to die for their faith. To some this may sound extreme but thousands of people have lost their life for the cause of Christ. I am not telling you that you need to be a martyr. I am simply pointing out a heart that so loves Jesus is willing to surrender all.

> "Greater love hath no man than this, that a man lay down his life for his friends" (John 15:13).

10. AVOID DELIBERATE SIN

Deliberate sin should be an obvious avoidance for everybody. Sin literally separates you from God.

> "His own iniquities shall take the wicked himself, and he shall be holden with the cords of his sins. He shall die without instruction; and in the greatness of his folly he shall go astray" (Proverbs 5:22-23).

11. MAINTAIN A FORGIVING HEART

As we have already studied in this handbook it is important to have a forgiving heart. When Peter asked Jesus how often he should forgive Jesus said, "Until seventy times seven" (Matthew 18:22). Most Bible scholars believe that means to forgive 490 times daily. The scripture also teaches us not to let any root of bitterness spring us in our lives.

> "Looking diligently lest any man fail of the grace of God; lest any root of bitterness springing up trouble you, and thereby many be defiled" (Hebrews 12:15).

12. TAKE HOLD OF YOUR THOUGHT LIFE

In my book *Imaginations, Dare to Win the Battle Against Your Mind*[1] I spend a great deal of time discussing the war against one's mind. Every vain imagination must be taken captive.

> "Casting down imaginations, and every high thing that exalteth itself against the knowledge of God, and bringing into captivity every thought to the obedience of Christ" (2 Corinthians 10:5).

I pray that this deliverance handbook, with the help of the Holy Spirit, has opened your eyes to an understanding of your authority in regards to deliverance. Everything that Jesus provided for us at Calvary has been given to us, including the anointing to set people free from demonic powers. The anointing has been given to remove burdens and destroy yokes. Let us not deprive this generation of the precious anointing for deliverance. For it is written,

> "Deliverance is the children's bread" (Matthew 15:26).

Next time you encounter demonic activity remember that you have been authorized to shout, "Come Out!"

Note

[1]Jonas Clark, "Imaginations, Dare to Win the Battle Against Your Mind," (Hallandale Beach, Fl. Spirit of Life Publications, www.jonasclark.com)

PRAYER FOR DELIVERANCE

Heavenly Father, I renounce and repent right now of any sins that I have committed both knowingly and unknowingly. I believe that Jesus died on the cross for my sins and that he rose again from the dead.

I repent of any rebellion, disobedience, unforgiveness, lust, pornography, perversion, witchcraft, abortion, divination, occult involvement, bitterness, idolatry, control or self righteousness. Thank you Jesus that I am washed clean by your precious blood.

I take authority over any demonic spirits that are attacking my life in the name of Jesus. Spirits of sickness, depression, oppression, insanity, familiar spirits, suicide, addictions, racism, divination, debt, destructive behavior and generational curses.

I execute authority by using the name of Jesus and bind any demonic assignments against myself, my marriage, family, children, grand children, and my job. Any assignments against my relationships, emotions and imaginations.

I bind every hex, curse, vex, assignment, spell, power, spoken words, Jezebel influences, religious spirits, legalism, Pharisee spirits, chains, cords, shackles, fetters, habits, roots, potions, spirit guides and evil helps.

I take back my will and submit thoroughly to the Lordship of my Savior and Redeemer Jesus Christ. He is my advocate, counselor, protector, mighty God, fortress and warrior.

I bind every spirit of death, destruction, confusion, instability, double-mindedness, pain, strife, anger, loneliness, sadness and anguish. I command all these demons to come out in the name of Jesus.

I thank you Jesus that whosoever calls on the name of the Lord shall be delivered. I am now free to serve you. I declare that greater is he that is in me than he that is in the world. Thank you Jesus that you are the author and finisher of my faith. Amen.

Invitation to Destiny

Are you hungry for more of God? In addition to preaching the Gospel around the world, we also pastor a powerful, Spirit-filled church in South Florida. The Spirit of God told us to build a church from which to send forth believers that could reach their cities and impact the nations for Jesus Christ.

Have you been searching for God only to find religion? Spirit of Life Ministries (SOLM) is a multi-cultural church where all races gather together in unity and cares for the needs of the whole family. Is something missing from your life? SOLM is a church where you can receive what you need from the Lord. We believe in divine healing, manifesting the gifts of the Spirit, prayer results, miracles, prosperity, finding purpose and making a difference. With God all things are possible.

Are you looking for a place to grow? SOLM is a new apostolic church with all five-fold ministry gifts operating. We have a prophetic call and mandate to equip, activate and release every believer into the work of the ministry according to Ephesians 4:11-12. We invite you to come and connect with your destiny and receive confirmation, impartation and activation for your life.

Come adventure with us,

Exposing Spiritual Witchcraft

How to overcome curses, demons, witchcraft and controlling power.

ISBN 1-886885-00-1

Spiritual witchcraft is probably attacking you – whether or not you know it. Every believer needs to learn how to recognize the weapons of witchcraft and be equipped with practical strategies to overcome it.

Spiritual witchcraft is the power of Satan. Its weapons are emotional manipulation, spiritual and religious control, isolation, soul ties, fear, confusion, loss of personal identity, sickness, depression and prophetic divination. Those caught in the snare of this spirit struggle throughout their Christian lives to remain stable. In order to successfully battle spiritual witchcraft you must thoroughly understand your rights as children of God because this demonic force craves to enslave those who are ignorant to the truth.

"I fought this spirit from April to November and won. So can you!"
– Author, Jonas Clark

To order Exposing Spiritual Witchcraft, log on to www.JonasClark.com or call 800.943.6490.

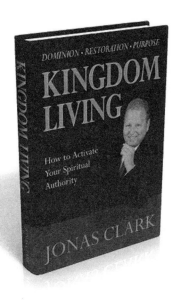

Easy Read Pocket-sized Books

Jezebel & Prophetic Ministry • Entering Prophetic Ministry
How Witchcraft Spirits Attack • Seeing What Others Can't
Unlocking Prophetic Imaginations

Healing Rejection & Emotional Abuse • Overcoming Dark Imaginations
What To Do When You Feel Like Giving Up • Prophecy Without
Permission • The Weapons of Your Warfare

More Titles: Avoiding Foreign Spirits • How Prophets Fail • Breaking Christian Witchcraft • Identifying Prophetic Spiritists • How Jezebel Hijacks Prophetic Ministry • Unlocking Your Spiritual Authority • Prophetic Confrontation

For more easy read Pocket-sized books
visit www.JonasClark.com
or call 800.943.6490.

Jonas Clark's Revolutionary Review Newsletter

Topic: Becoming a King in God's Kingdom

You double opted-in to receive Jonas Clark's Revolutionary Review Newsletter. You subscribed as webmaster@jonasclark.com.

Jonas prays daily for his partners in Christ.

View this e-mail in your browser.

JONAS CLARK'S
REVOLUTIONARY REVIEW
INFORMING, EQUIPPING & EMPOWERING EVERY BELIEVER

Home | Blog | Global Cause Network | Book Reviews | Bookstore

Becoming a King in God's Kingdom

By Jonas Clark

Kingship is acting on your spiritual authority to invade, occupy and influence the world around you. It is fulfilling the first great commission to "multiply, produce, increase, subdue and take dominion." Today, however, it seems everyone wants to be a prophet and no one a king. What good is a low-level prophetic word while the wicked continue to rule over God's people?

Anything dealing with prophetic ministry is hot. I have a pocket-sized book out entitled "Entering Prophetic Ministry" that people are ordering like hot cakes. In this book I write about how to enter prophetic ministry. It seems everyone wants to be a prophet. The danger

GOVERNING BELIEVERS:

Your apostolic nature is found in three words: **building, restoring and governing.** These three ruling properties

Receive bi-weekly FREE articles from Jonas Clark to equip you for your destiny.Read present truth articles on topics such as apostolic ministry, spritual warfare, deliverance, prophetic ministry, Kingdom living and more.

Sign up today @
www.JonasClark.com

JONAS CLARK MINISTRIES

Biblical answers you've been searching for...

From the revolutionary teaching ministry of Jonas Clark,
Topics written with you in mind including, apostolic and prophetic issues, deliverance, healing and Spirit-led living. Great for your library or a gift for pastors, teachers and students of the Word.

30 PIECES OF SILVER
Discerning religious spirits and entering the Kingdom.

ISBN 1-116885-18-4

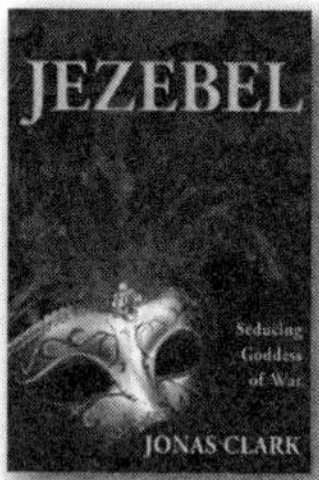

JEZEBEL: Seducing Goddess of War
Recognize this spirit's manipulative ways and break free from its controlling powers.

ISBN 1-886885-04-4

EXPOSING SPIRITUAL WITCHCRAFT
How to overcome curses, demons, witchcraft and controlling powers.

ISBN 1-886885-00-1

LIFE AFTER REJECTION:
God's path to emotional healing. Start prospering over rejection and reclaim your life from fear.

ISBN 1-886885-22-2

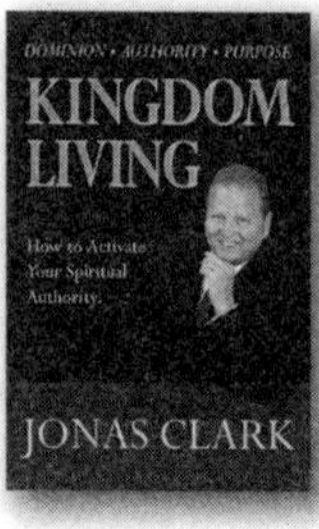

KINGDOM LIVING
How to activate your spiritual authority
Discover dominion restoration and purpose in the Kingdom of God.

ISBN 1-886885-21-4

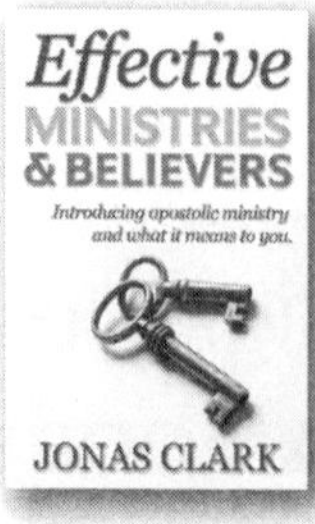

EFFECTIVE MINISTRIES AND BELIEVERS
Introducing the apostolic ministry and what it means to you.

ISBN 1-886885-25-7

New Release!
JEZABEL, Diosa Seductora De La Guerra
No toleres a Jezabel... ¡equípate y gane sobre este espíritu hoy!

ISBN 1-886885-28-1

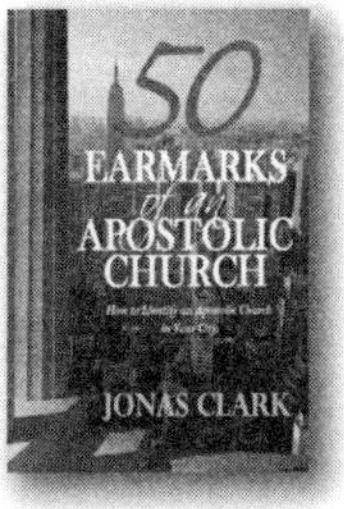

50 EARMARKS OF AN APOSTOLIC CHURCH
How to identify an apostolic church in your city.

ISBN 1-886885-06-0

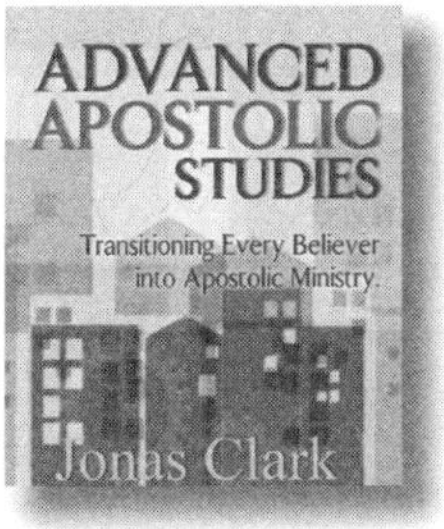

ADVANCED APOSTOLIC STUDIES
Transitioning every believer into apostolic ministry.

ISBN 1-886885-17-6

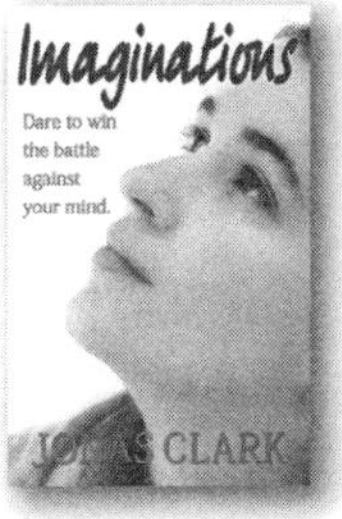

IMAGINATIONS: **Dare to Win the Battle Against Your Mind.**
Practical proven strategies cast down evil thoughts and be free.

ISBN 1-886885-26-5

EXTREME PROPHETIC STUDIES
Learn how to run with the prophets.

ISBN 1-886885-19-2

Now featuring Books, MP3s, CDs, and Videos.

g on to www.JonasClark.com for Internet specials
nd for FREE bonus offers or call 800.943.6490.

Jonas Clark
Hallandale Beach, FL